nine lives

kent zimmerman

Cover design is from an original
silk screen by Brad Harvey.

ISBN 978-1-967361-81-6 (Paperback)
ISBN 978-1-967361-82-3 (Ebook)

Inquiries and Book Orders
should be addressed to:

Leavitt Peak Press
17901 Pioneer Blvd Ste L #298,
Artesia, California 90701
Phone #: 2092191548

"I flingi on the wind I Winnie o the blue sky"

M. Zimmerman

A MEMORY
OF CATCHES
IN WORD WORLD III
A BALLET
FOR LETTING GO
OF O
O RHY THM
OF WOODWINDS
PLAYING

A MEMORY

far into the dark
father cut apart
the skin of an animal
to free them

the howling was of pain
and of joy

they would never forget it

OF CATCHES

into the reaches

we are the catches

hold on!

IN WORD WORLD III

see

see what

see what i see
i saw a word see

so it seems

i said i saw
a see saw

words
are like a see saw

if you see what i mean

A BALLET

mother told them once
about a girl who loved to dance
and of a man from far away
so far he came
from where he sat

in their travels round
they gave the world the ballet

FOR LETTING GO

(a poem of appearance)

the body aspires
in the workings of it

yet it sits
not letting go

things are on hold
until they fly up
into the face of it

deep in the veins
are the grains of it

whenever it moves
it opens the mouth of it

everything else moves too

OF O

soft lights overhead
two sister moons

      go with her

   everywhere

and she puts on a loose dress

O RHY THM

do waka do
waka do do do

OF WOODWINDS

from a field
slight vibrations ahead

there a strange
wood song we played
on strings waves and air

growing bigger
we saw trees
with grey hair
follicles gone white
at limbs end
in light of moons
and stars

the message departing
was the cue to the other
telling in sleep
of another
this coming and going forever

PLAYING

unknown rooms and faces

exchange for a new name
say the name is your own

later with the same faces
change the face for other faces

(chorus)
moving about the room
amass and go home

PostScript I: META POSTAL EXPRESSION

Postcard book soon to be published 2025
m black to blue, it pokes good, obliterate o,
GOPASSGO

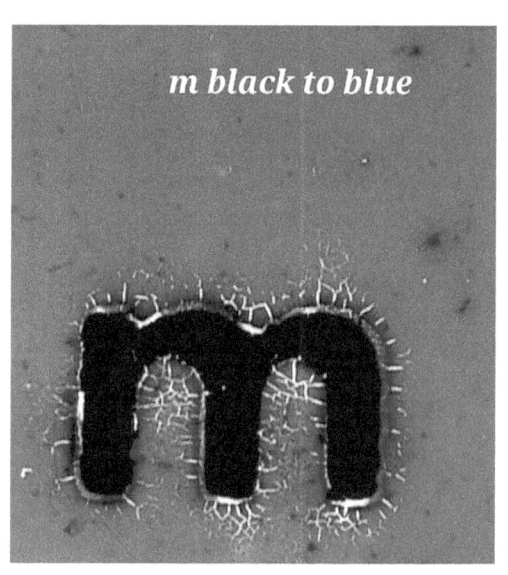

m black to blue

...obliterates o

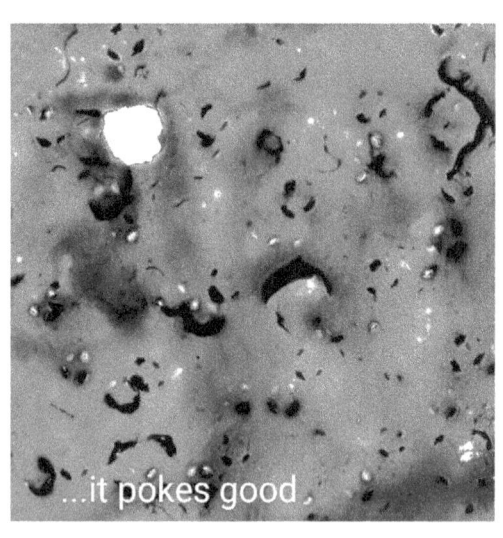

...it pokes good

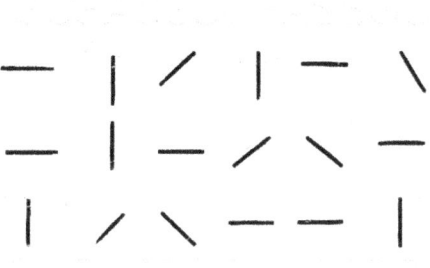

PostScript II: ARCHETYPE RULES

by M. Zimmerman

THE HAT GAME

we are going to have drama lessons
tonight after dinner

(each person will draw and mime one of the
following)

BEING QUITE SHSH
TOKING
SQRTING WATR AT PEPFUL
BIRDS FLINGI IN THE SKY
MAKING DOWE
PIKING FLOWRS
PETHING A CAT

RGUING
SLEPING
TAKING A BATH
JOLEY

RAKUN

www.ingramcontent.com/pod-product-compliance
Lightning Source LLC
Chambersburg PA
CBHW051253120626
46547CB00014B/1933